Fast break

Play ball

Jump ball

Ready for practice

Tying laces securely

Overplaying an opponent

Triple threat position

DK SUPERGUIDES

Basket and backboard

BASKETBALL

CHRIS MULLIN

with
Brian Coleman

Smart dribbler

Safe passing

Moving to receive the ball

Shooting for the basket

Basic basketball stance

DK PUBLISHING, INC.

DK www.dk.com

A DORLING KINDERSLEY BOOK

DK www.dk.com

Project editors Bernadette Crowley, Stella Love **Art editor** Lesley Betts
Photography Susanna Price
Picture research Rachel Leach
Production Charlotte Traill
Deputy editorial director Sophie Mitchell
Deputy art director Miranda Kennedy

The young basketball players
Martin Anastasi, Lauren Kent, Kieron Parris,
Chelsee Stewart, Mark Theinmaung, Lendel Wright

First American Edition, 2000
2 4 6 8 10 9 7 5 3 1
Published in the United States by
Dorling Kindersley Publishing, Inc.
95 Madison Avenue
New York, NY 10016

ISBN: 0-7894-5426-2
Color reproduction by Colourscan, Singapore
Printed and bound in Italy by L.E.G.O.

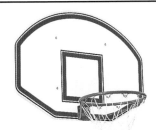

Contents

To all young players

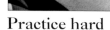

Here I am playing in the NBA for my team, the Golden State Warriors.

"WHEN I WAS just starting to play basketball, the most important lesson I learned was discipline, and how to apply it. If you work hard and follow the rules, you will learn the difference between doing things the right way and doing things the wrong way. Playing basketball has taught me how to work well with others, too, and I've become friends with my opponents as well as my teammates. From the time I started playing in the schoolyards of Brooklyn, New York, throughout my NBA career and my time on the US Olympic "Dream Team," I have always played hard. But I've enjoyed every minute. I hope that you will enjoy reading this book and have as much fun as I have had playing basketball."

Practice hard
As a young player you need to develop all aspects of your game. Although people compliment me on my shooting techniques, I have worked hard to become proficient in dribbling, passing, defending, and other team play skills.

LaPhonso Ellis and Robert Pack of the Denver Nuggets are trying to block my shot.

Olympic games
I had a fantastic time with the "Dream Team" at the Barcelona Olympics in 1992. This was my second Olympic Games – I played in the Los Angeles Olympics in 1984 while I was still in college.

See how I concentrate when preparing to take a shot at the basket.

Here I am trying to get two more points for the Warriors.

Tough opponents
When playing for the Golden State Warriors in the NBA, I have to compete against big and athletic opponents. One skill I have learned is the ability to ignore the efforts of defenders trying to distract me as I shoot at the basket.

History of basketball

BASKETBALL was invented in December 1891 by Dr. James Naismith, a teacher at the YMCA International Training School in Massachusetts. Dr. Naismith wanted to relieve the boredom of his students during winter physical education classes when the weather kept everyone indoors. He had two fruit baskets nailed to the balconies at each end of a gym, found a soccer ball, and set out some rules that are the same basic rules of the game today.

Dr. James Naismith
Dr. Naismith, who was born in Canada in 1861, lived long enough to see the game he invented played throughout the world. The spread in basketball's popularity was largely due to the efforts of the YMCA.

Where it all started
The first game of basketball was played in a basement gymnasium in this building. There was only one basket scored and a stepladder was used to retrieve the ball from the fruit basket.

The US team members included seven players from the Universal Picture Studios team in Hollywood.

The caged game
In the early days of professional basketball, the court was enclosed in netting to separate the players from the spectators. This is why basketball is sometimes called the "caged game."

Berlin Olympics
Basketball first became an official Olympic sport at the Berlin Olympics in 1936. Teams from 21 countries competed. The US team won the tournament, and their gold medals were presented by Dr. Naismith.

Bob Cousy
Bob Cousy is one of the greatest players in basketball history. He played for the Boston Celtics in the 1960s, when they won nine NBA Championships in a row.

Michael Jordan
Michael Jordan of the Chicago Bulls is one of the modern game's most outstanding players. He was one of my teammates in the "Dream Team."

Michael Jordan is known as a great jumper and ball handler.

A German defender tries to prevent Michael Jordan from taking a shot.

The Dream Team
The Olympic Games was originally a competition for amateurs. In the 1992 Olympics in Barcelona, Spain, the professional basketball players from the NBA were allowed to compete for the first time. I was very excited to be included in the team selected to represent the US, which won the gold medal. This Olympic team was known as the "Dream Team" because it contained all the star players in American basketball.

Starting basketball

WHEN YOU START playing basketball, you can wear comfortable, loose-fitting clothes and basketball shoes. If you progress to play in a team, you will have to wear an official uniform – shorts and a sleeveless shirt. The most important item of clothing is your footwear. Your shoes need to support your ankles and have nonslip soles. They must also cushion your feet to absorb the impact of the vigorous jumps and landings that are a part of the game. Basic basketball equipment consists simply of a ball and a basket with a backboard. The game ball is round, and when it is dropped from a height of 6 ft (1.8 m) it should bounce to a height of about 4 ft 2 in (1.3 m).

Playing uniform
Each player on a basketball team wears the same color uniform. The shirts and shorts do not have to match, but each must be one solid color only, although they may have different-colored trim. The shirts are numbered on the front and back, and no two players can have the same number. In professional games, the shirts often have the player's name on the back and the team logo on the front.

This material is lightweight and has holes to allow air circulation.

Your uniform should be loose so it does not restrict your movement.

Make sure your shoes are big enough for you to wear thick socks. This will prevent you from getting blisters.

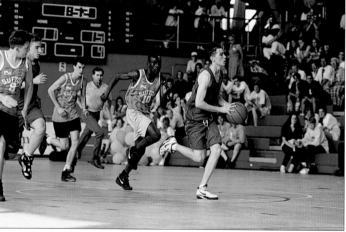

Playing for fun
As you develop as a player, you may want to join a local team. As a team member, you will be guided by a coach who will make sure you develop your skills correctly. You will also have an opportunity to play in regular organized competitive games. In this picture, two junior teams are competing in a local tournament.

Basic equipment

The backboard is made of either wood or a thick, rigid type of plastic.

Tracksuit

Wear a tracksuit when you are warming up or sitting on the substitutes' bench. There should be zippers in the pant legs so that you can remove them quickly over your basketball shoes.

Your tracksuit can have your team's name and logo on it.

You can carry your clothing in a duffel bag.

Net

The rim should be 10 ft (3.05 m) above floor level.

Warm up

You must warm up your muscles before a game. If you are cold when you start playing, you can easily pull a muscle.

Practice rim and backboard

If you have a basket at home or at school, you can develop your shooting skills. You can also play a game, even if there is only you and one other person.

Shoe with high ankle support

Shoe with lower ankle support

Footwear

You can wear shoes with a high or low ankle support – most modern players wear shoes that support their ankles. During a game, turning, jumping, and stopping put a lot of strain on your joints.

The ball is made of eight shaped panels.

The ball

The ball has an outer casing made of either leather, rubber, or a synthetic material. It should weigh between 20-22 oz (567-650 g) and have a circumference of 29½-30¾ in (75-78 cm).

Make sure your laces are tied securely.

The basketball court

ONE OF THE reasons basketball is so popular around the world is that it is a very simple game. All you need to play is a ball, a basket, and a smooth floor. You may have started playing the game at your school or in a local playground. Perhaps you dream of playing in a major basketball arena, with a special wooden floor, glass backboards, and thousands of spectators. But whether basketball is played in a playground or on a professional court, the game still consists of controlling a ball on a smooth floor.

Professional court

The NBA is the world's leading professional basketball league, with teams playing in major arenas throughout the US. The arena in this picture is the ARCO, home of the Sacramento Kings, in California. The ARCO arena seats more than 17,000 spectators. The game in play is between the Kings and the Los Angeles Lakers. The scorer's table and the team benches are on the right-hand side of this picture.

This large four-sided scoreboard hangs over the center of the court.

The scoreboard shows that the Lakers lead the Kings by 83 points to 70.

Spectators can also see the game on this large screen.

ARCO ARENA

The King's team logo

Three referees (dressed here in dark pants and gray tops) control the game in the NBA.

The restricted area is painted blue for easy identification.

Shot clock is blank because a shot has been taken.

The backboard is transparent so that spectators behind it can see the game.

Backboard and shot clock

The backboard measures 6 ft (1.8 m) across and 3½ ft (1.05 m) down, and is padded at the bottom to prevent injury to tall players. The shot clock checks the time that a team is in possession of the ball before a player takes a shot. In the NBA a team must shoot within 24 seconds of gaining possession, and in FIBA (International Basketball Federation) rules, within 30 seconds of gaining possession. The shot clock counts down to zero and is blanked out when a shot is taken because neither team has the ball. If a team fails to take a shot within the time limit, it loses possession.

The Game

Winning a game

A game is won by the team that scores the most points. Points are scored by putting the ball through the basket.

Game duration

In FIBA rules, a game is divided into two 20-minute halves, while in the NBA it is divided into four quarters of 12 minutes each. There are many stoppages during a game and a full game usually lasts about 90 minutes. The visiting team chooses which end it will attack for the first half of the game, and the teams swap ends at halftime.

Overtime

If the teams' scores are equal at full time, five minutes of overtime is played. If neither team has won after the five minutes, further five-minute periods of overtime are played until one or the other team wins.

Charged time-outs

Each team has a coach, and during a game coaches can ask for play to stop temporarily – in the FIBA, four times per game and once in each overtime; in the NBA, nine times per game and three times in each overtime. These stoppages are called charged time-outs. They can last in the FIBA for a maximum of one minute; in the NBA, there are two 20-second time-outs and seven 100-second time-outs.

Substitutes

A player on the court can be substituted for if the coach wants to change tactics or rest a tired or injured player. On a substitution, the substitute reports to the scorer, and when the game clock operator stops the clock, an official beckons the substitute to exchange places with a player on the court. A player who has been replaced can be substituted back into the game.

Court markings, teams, and officials

A basketball game involves two teams of five players. In addition, each team has substitutes (from five to seven substitutes depending on the league) who sit on the team bench with coaches and other team officials. Between the two team benches is the scorer's table. At each end of the scorer's table there are seats for substitutes who are waiting for an opportunity to enter the game (the NBA does not have these seats). There are some differences in the playing rules used in the NBA, the NCAA (National Collegiate Athletic Association, which runs the college game in the US), and the FIBA. One major difference between these leagues is the way the court is marked, which is indicated in the diagram below. Another difference is that in international basketball the game is controlled by two referees, and in the US by three floor officials.

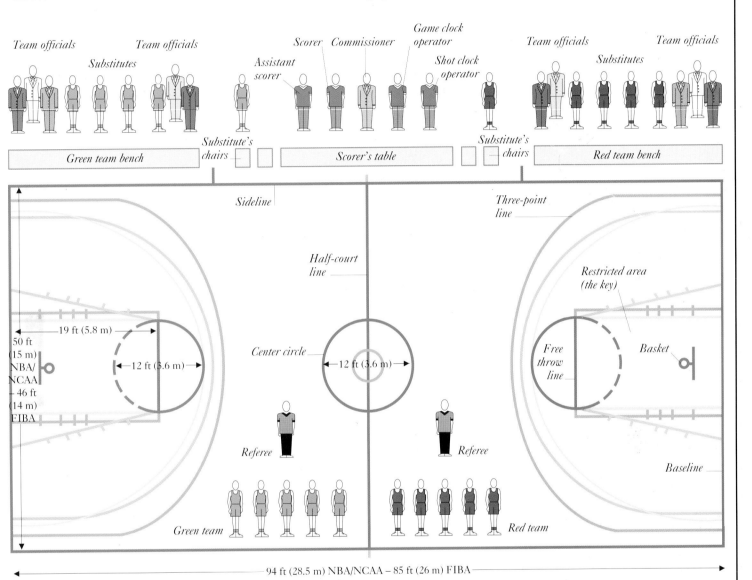

Key to officials and court diagram

Statistician – keeps a record of shots taken and scored, etc.

Assistant coach – assists the coach

Scorer – keeps a record of the score and of fouls committed

Shot clock operator – restarts the shot clock on each new possession

Doctor/ physiotherapist – treats players' injuries

Coach – trains the team and directs play during the game

Commissioner – a match supervisor in FIBA rules basketball

Green team – team of five players on court and five substitutes

Team manager – organizes team uniforms and travel

Assistant scorer – assists the scorer

Game clock operator – operates the game clock

Red team – team of five players on court and five substitutes

NCAA court markings

NBA court markings

FIBA court markings

Boundary lines and half-court line – the same on all courts

Dribbling

DRIBBLING IS one of the basic skills you will need to master as a basketball player. Dribbling allows you to move with the ball to a new position on the court by bouncing the ball off the floor. If you are going to become a good basketball player, you will need to learn when to dribble and when not to. You should not dribble the ball every time you receive it. This would stop your team from playing effectively. Dribbling is only used for moving the ball up the court from defense to attack; moving to a good position to take a shot at the basket; and getting away from an opponent to find space to pass the ball to a teammate.

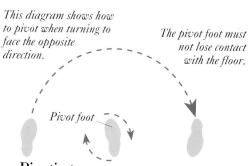

This diagram shows how to pivot when turning to face the opposite direction.

The pivot foot must not lose contact with the floor.

Pivot foot

Pivoting

When you come to a stop with the ball, you are allowed to change the direction you are facing. This is called pivoting. When you pivot, you keep one foot on the ground (the pivot foot) while you step with the other foot. You may pivot in any direction.

Basic dribbling

You control the ball when dribbling by using your wrist and fingers. You may use only one hand at a time when dribbling, but you can change hands as often as you want. Using your forearm, wrist, and fingers, push the ball firmly down to the floor. Learn to control the height and speed of the bounce of the ball, varying it from chest height to below knee height. Try moving around as you dribble, too, changing hands and direction as you move.

1 When you start dribbling from a standstill, you must release the ball for the first bounce before both feet leave the floor. As you dribble, feel the ball with your fingers. Try not to touch the ball with the palms of your hands.

2 Push the ball down to the floor with a flowing wrist and finger action. Do not slap the ball. Your wrist and fingers need to be flexible.

Keep your head up so that you can see the other players on the court.

Keep the ball close to your body, otherwise an opponent might steal the ball as it bounces.

Protecting the ball Remember to protect the ball from defenders by dribbling it on the side of your body away from your opponent.

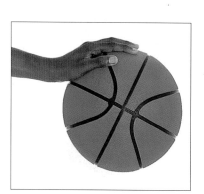

Dribbling hand
You control the ball by spreading your fingers comfortably, touching as much of the ball as possible. Your hand should touch the top of the ball except when you change direction with the ball.

Face the basket
Whenever you get the ball you should immediately pivot to face the basket. This is also known as "squaring up to the basket."

Personal space
Each player has a personal space, a cylinder-shaped area around the body about as wide as the shoulders. It stretches from the floor to the ceiling. If an opponent makes contact with you inside your cylinder, it could be a foul.

Hold your head up throughout the pivot.

Use your body as a shield to protect the ball from a defender.

Your back should be straight.

Keep your pivot foot on the same point on the floor.

Keep your knees bent for good balance.

Take short steps as you turn for better control.

3 As the ball comes back up, spread your fingers to receive it. At first, practice dribbling while standing still so you get used to the feel of the bouncing ball.

4 Now test yourself. See if you can dribble the ball without looking at it. It is essential that you learn to do this so that you can always see the position of other players as you dribble.

Dribbling rule
Once you have stopped dribbling, you are not permitted to start again until the ball has been played by another player. If you do start dribbling again, it is a violation of the rules called a double dribble.

Keep your arm close to your body.

You must learn to dribble by feeling the ball rather than looking at it.

Practice dribbling against an opponent who is trying to steal the ball from you.

You may take as many steps as you like when you are dribbling the ball.

Drive to score

YOU CAN CLAIM to have mastered the skill of dribbling when you can successfully dribble against an opponent. You will often be closely guarded by a defender when you are dribbling and you must be constantly aware of their position. Remember that you are dribbling to try to move past your opponent closer to the basket. You will need to develop equal dribbling skills with both hands. In addition, you will need to be able to protect the bouncing ball from an opponent by putting your body between the defender and the ball.

Dribble behind the back

Dribbling the ball behind your back is an advanced skill that requires lots of practice. Dribble the ball out to your side and move it behind you. Pushing the top and rear of the ball, bounce it to the other hand. Your goal is to perform this dribble while moving.

Fake and drive

When you have the ball and you are closely guarded, try a "fake and drive." A fake is when you pretend you are going to make one move, and when the opponent falls for your fake, you do something different. For example, you could fake a shot and then dribble to the basket. A drive is an aggressive dribbling move toward the basket.

Arms raised to defend a possible shot at the basket.

You can start the fake and drive by pretending to shoot.

When you square up to the basket, use the basic basketball stance.

Look in the direction you are pretending to move in.

Your defender has moved to the right and is looking at the ball, waiting to stop your drive.

Make this first step a short jab in the direction of the fake.

1 When you receive the ball, stand so you have good balance. The basic basketball stance is with feet spread about shoulder-width apart, knees bent, hips slightly tilted, back straight, head up, and weight evenly spread on your feet.

2 Take a fake step in one direction as though you intend to dribble past your defender. Keep the step short, and make sure you keep the ball under control. The defender will move to cover your anticipated drive.

Reverse dribble

Use the reverse dribble when you want to beat a defender who has moved into your path. With this move you make a quick change of direction, switching hands as you dribble and turning your back on your opponent to go in the opposite direction.

Always be aware of what your opponent is doing.

Change dribbling hands as you turn.

When you turn, use a long step to go past your opponent.

Step toward the defender and pivot to turn your back on your opponent.

Pivot foot

1 If you are dribbling with your right hand and a defender has moved into your path, bounce the ball to your left hand as you start to turn your back on the defender.

2 Turn on your left foot as the ball touches your left hand and step to the right as you quickly rotate. You will now have your back to your opponent.

3 Continue to dribble the ball with your left hand as you move toward the basket, leaving your opponent behind you.

Stopping dribbling
Learn to pick the ball up as you stop dribbling and move directly into a shot or a pass to a teammate.

Take the ball in your right hand as you prepare to dribble.

Keep your hand behind the ball so you can dribble it forward.

The defender is off balance and will take a moment to recover.

Keep your head up to see the other players around you.

Be careful not to make body contact with your defender as you pass him. This could be a foul.

This second step should be long so you move past your defender with a single step.

3 While the defender is moving to the right, step to his left with the same foot you used for the fake step. This should be a long step. As you take the step, release the ball to start the drive. Make sure you pass close to your opponent and move toward the basket.

4 Continue the drive, taking the straightest route to the basket. Remember that other defenders can step in to stop you. Keep your head up as you dribble so that you can see the basket and the movements of all the players.

Passing

To PLAY GOOD BASKETBALL, you must learn how to deliver and receive a pass. Once a team has possession of the ball, it is important to keep possession through safe passing. The fastest way of moving the ball up the court is by passing it, so if you have a choice, you should pass rather than dribble the ball. There are several different types of passes. You can decide which one to use by judging the game situation and by watching the position and movements of teammates and opponents.

Chest pass

The chest pass is a two-handed pass that is made only when there is no defender between you and the receiver. Start this pass with the ball held in both hands in front of your chest. This is called the triple threat position because from this point, you could do one of three things – either shoot, dribble, or pass.

Passing distance
The ideal time for this pass is when the passer and the receiver are about 11½-15 ft (3.5-4.5 m) apart.

Overhead pass

When you are guarded closely by an opponent, it is best to make an overhead pass, particularly if your opponent is shorter than you.

Hold the ball in front of your head.

Defender closely guards opponent.

1 Start the pass by holding the ball above head height. The ball should be above your forehead and held with both hands. Keep your eyes fixed on your target.

Hands point in the direction of the pass.

Be aware that your opponent may jump up and block your pass.

2 Make the pass with a vigorous flick of your wrists and fingers so that the ball goes in a swift, straight line to your teammate.

Moving free to receive

If you are being guarded by an opponent and you want to receive the ball, you must free yourself from your defender for at least an instant. You can achieve this by stepping toward your defender and then making a quick change of direction, moving out to receive the ball.

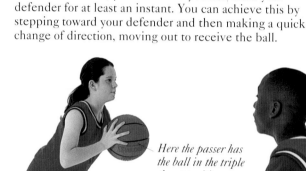

Here the passer has the ball in the triple threat position.

The passer pivots, looking for an opportunity to throw the ball.

1 The passer is looking at the movement of her teammates around her. The potential receiver, red number 4, is closely guarded by a defender. He steps between the defender's legs and then quickly steps out away from the defender.

Signal to the passer
Be sure to watch the ball at all times and indicate clearly to the passer where you want to catch the ball.

The receiver must keep his eyes on the ball.

The move begins with the receiver stepping with his right foot between the defender's legs.

The receiver quickly steps away from the defender with his left foot.

Flex your wrists backward.

1 Hold the ball in both hands with your thumbs behind it and your fingers along its sides. Do not touch the ball with the palms of your hands.

Stand in the basic basketball stance.

2 Make the pass by extending your arms sharply in the direction of the receiver. Move your body in the direction of the pass.

Make sure you have a firm grip on the ball.

Keep your elbows tucked in.

3 Release the ball as your arms straighten by flicking your wrists forward. When first practicing, step forward one pace as you make the pass.

Keep your eyes on your target.

Your fingers should point in the direction of the throw.

Take one step forward.

Good passing
An effective pass is one received by a teammate when and where they want the ball.

2 With a quick change of direction, number 4 puts his opponent into a poor position for intercepting the pass. As number 4 moves clear, he signals for the ball with his hands outstretched.

Use both hands when catching or passing the ball.

You may find it easier to lose your defender if you start walking slowly toward him, and then quickly change direction, running to receive the ball.

Take a long first step.

The defender has been taken by surprise.

The receiver has successfully freed himself from the defender.

The defender chases the receiver to continue guarding him.

3 The receiver takes the ball in both hands while on the move. After catching the ball, he should pivot to face the basket and prepare either to shoot, dribble, or pass.

More passing skills

O NE IMPORTANT passing skill is being able to recognize and create passing lanes. A passing lane is a route along which you can safely pass a ball to a teammate. In addition, you need to learn both how to pick the ball up as you stop dribbling, ready to pass it, and how to receive the ball legally (within the rules). The rules of the game state that you may only take one full pace while holding the ball, and if you are about to receive a pass, for instance, you will probably be moving. There are two methods that you can use to stop with the ball – the jump stop and the stride stop.

Control of the ball
In this picture Isiah Thomas has taken control of the ball. His knees are bent and his head is up so that he can see the game action in front of him. From this position he can see a teammate become free, and prepare to release an overhead pass down the court.

Bounce pass
If you are being guarded by a tall opponent, or if your defender's arms are raised, it is difficult to find a passing lane for a chest or overhead pass. In this situation the best pass to use is a bounce pass. This is made by bouncing the ball off the floor toward the receiver.

Hold your head up.

The defender has his arms raised to prevent a chest pass being made.

Keep your back straight.

Watch the ball as it bounces to your teammate.

1 When you see a receiver signaling for a bounce pass, quickly bend and push the ball toward him. Make sure you can clearly see where you are aiming the ball. You should bounce the ball at a spot two-thirds of the way between you and the receiver. Think of skidding the ball off the floor rather than bouncing it, since this will make it move faster.

You may pivot to step to the side of your opponent to make the pass.

Stride stop

If you receive the ball while in midair, you are allowed to take only two steps, called the two-count rhythm, to stop legally. You may use the stride stop when you receive a pass moving at speed or as you stop dribbling.

Keep your head up.

When you come to a stop, you may pass or shoot the ball.

Hold the ball in the triple threat position.

1 Catch the ball while you are in midair. As you travel forward, you will land on one foot, which will become your pivot foot. This is the first count of the two-count rhythm.

2 Keep your landing foot firmly on the ground as you bring your second foot forward in a normal running action.

Landing foot

Bring your second foot forward.

3 Bring down your other foot. This is the second count. You should finish the stop in a good balanced position with both feet flat on the floor, one foot in front of the other.

Pivot foot

Keep your head held high and your eyes fixed on the ball.

Your back should be straight.

Short passes
The longer the pass, the more time a defender has to move to intercept the ball. Therefore keep your passes short – 11½-15 ft (3.5-4.5 m) long.

Hold your hands low, ready to receive the ball.

2 If you are the receiver, signal where you want the ball. Always be aware of the movements of your opponents. The bounce pass is slower than other passes, which can make it easier for opponents to intercept.

Signaling to receive
If you want to receive the ball and can see a passing lane under an opponent, you should signal for a bounce pass by holding your hands low.

Jump stop

In a jump stop you land on the floor with both feet at the same time, having caught the ball while you are in midair. The great advantage of this stop is that you can choose either foot as your pivot foot.

Hold your head high.

Keep the ball close to your body.

1 Catch the ball in midair. As you come down to land, make sure both your feet touch the floor at the same time.

Feet are ready to land at the same time.

2 Once you have landed correctly, you can pivot on either foot. Remember that once you have started to pivot on one foot, you cannot change to pivot on the other foot.

Stand in the triple threat position.

Keep your feet shoulder-width apart for good balance.

Shooting skills

A BASKETBALL GAME is won by the team with the most points, and you can only get points by shooting the ball through the basket. Every team member can score, so developing your shooting skills is vital. There are different types of shots, and you will need to learn several different techniques if you are to become a regular scorer for your team. The type of shot you take will depend on your situation. If you are standing still with the ball and are within shooting range, you can take a set shot or a jump shot. If you are able to dribble up to the basket, you can take a layup shot.

The set shot

You will be stationary when you make a set shot, so your stance is very important. Stand with your knees slightly bent and the ball held in front of your chest, just under your chin. Hold your shooting hand behind and slightly under the ball, with your fingers spread and pointing upward.

Hold the ball with both hands.

If you are a right-handed shooter, place your right foot slighly farther forward than your left foot.

The layup

You should perform a layup when you are on the move, after catching a pass or when dribbling toward the basket. This sequence of pictures shows a player moving to take a layup. He has approached the basket from the right, having dribbled the ball with his right hand.

Holding the ball
When you hold the ball for a shot, do not touch the ball with the palms of your hands, use only your fingers.

3 Your left foot is your takeoff foot for your jump upward and toward the basket. You should start lifting the ball up in front of you as you start your shooting action.

1 When you are within range of the basket for a layup, gather the ball in both hands while both your feet are off the ground. Bring your right foot down to land.

Move at a good pace.

Keep your eyes on your target.

2 Look up to the basket as your left foot comes forward to land. Remember that you are only allowed to take two steps when you are holding the ball.

Your left foot takes the second, and final step.

Bring your right leg forward as you prepare to jump from your left foot.

Your arms should reach up toward the basket.

Release the ball with a strong flick of your wrists and fingers.

Make the action one continuous movement.

For longer shots, you may lift your feet off the floor.

As you start the shot, straighten your legs.

Releasing the ball
You must reach up so that you release the ball as close to the basket as possible.

The flight of the ball should continue to a target point on the backboard.

If you hit the correct spot on the backboard, the ball will rebound into the basket.

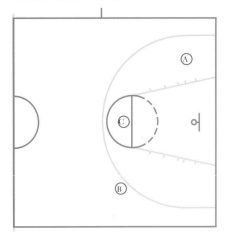

Take your left hand away from the ball just before you shoot with your right hand.

Your shooting arm should be fully stretched.

Point the fingers of your shooting hand upward.

Stretch up your arms.

Concentrate on the target until your shot goes in.

Jump off the foot opposite your shooting hand.

Jump as high as you can.

6 Gently guide the ball up toward the target so that it drops softly into the basket. If you are a beginner, move toward the basket at an angle of 45° to the backboard. You will see a gap between the hoop and the backboard through which it is easier to aim the ball at the backboard. Try varying your angle of approach as you become more skilled.

Scoring points

The number of points you get for a basket depends on where you took the shot from. A field goal (a basket scored from open play as opposed to a penalty shot) taken from point A, within the three point line, is worth two points. A field goal scored by a player at point B, with both feet behind the three point line, is worth three points. A free throw (a penalty shot awarded for a rule infringement) taken from point C is worth 1 point.

4 To get more lift when you jump, drive your right knee upward. Hold the ball with your shooting hand behind and slightly under it. Your other hand should be at the side of the ball, giving it support.

5 Just before releasing the ball, you should be at full stretch and be holding the ball as high as possible. Aim the ball at a point just inside the top corner closest to you of the small rectangle on the backboard. If you hit that target, the ball should rebound into the basket.

More shots

SHOOTING IS probably the most exciting and entertaining part of basketball. You should shoot whenever you have a good opportunity, but you must learn to judge when an opportunity really is good. Remember that the ingredients of a good shot include being on balance, facing the basket, having the ball under control, and being able to concentrate on the basket. It will help if you develop a positive attitude toward scoring. Think you are going to score, and you are more likely to succeed.

Slam dunk
The slam dunk, being performed here by Pervis Ellison, is the most spectacular shot in basketball. This is the ultimate layup shot, in which a player jumps so high that he or she can push the ball down into the basket. You need to be tall or a very good jumper to make this shot. When dunking, you are not allowed to grasp the rim. This rule was written to keep players from accidentally breaking backboards.

The jump shot
The most important shot in modern basketball is the jump shot. It is a quick shot in which the shooter jumps vertically and releases the ball near the top of the jump. It is a difficult shot for a defender to intercept because the ball is released when the shooter is high in the air.

Your fingers should point upward.

Keep the elbow of your shooting arm directly beneath the ball.

Point your feet toward the basket.

The defender has his knees bent in his defensive stance.

1 Your starting position for a jump shot is facing the basket, feet flat on the floor about shoulder-width apart, and knees bent. It is vital that both your feet are pointing at the basket as you take this shot.

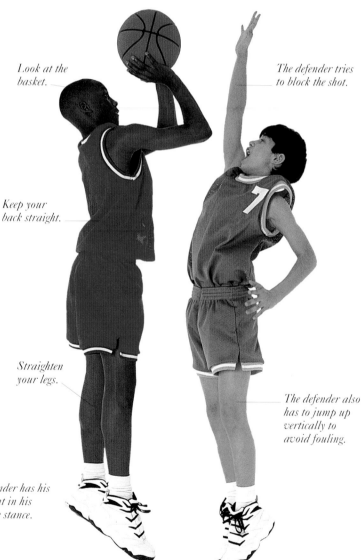

Look at the basket.

Keep your back straight.

Straighten your legs.

The defender tries to block the shot.

The defender also has to jump up vertically to avoid fouling.

2 From this starting position, jump upward off both feet. As you jump, lift the ball past your face to a position in front of your forehead. In this position, your view of the basket is underneath the ball.

Hook shot

In this picture David Robinson of the San Antonio Spurs is taking a hook shot. Use this shot when you are near the basket but have a defender between you and the basket. Take one step parallel to the basket with the opposite foot to your shooting hand. The shoulder of your non-shooting arm should point to the basket. As you jump, bring up your shooting arm and release the ball at full stretch. You remain between the defender and the ball throughout the shot.

Hold on to the follow-through.

Jump rhythm
Jump first and then shoot in a jump shot, releasing the ball during the pause at the top of your jump.

Concentrate on scoring and ignore the defender.

You should land on the same spot you took off from.

3 When you approach the top of your jump, push your arms upward and release the ball with a vigorous flick of your wrists toward the basket. Follow the shot through with your arms and hands and hold on to the follow-through until the ball hits the rim.

Fake and drive

If you are closely guarded, do not shoot. Instead, you can fake a shot and then drive toward the basket, perhaps to make a layup.

1 Face the basket and look up at it with the ball in the triple threat position, as if you are going to shoot. Your defender may raise her arms and move closer to you.

Position yourself as if you are going to shoot.

Wait until the defender has fallen for your fake before driving to basket.

The defender has jumped to block a shot.

2 Fake to shoot, and as the defender jumps to block your shot, quickly drive past her to the basket. This fake and drive is sometimes called an "up and under."

Take a very long step on your first movement.

3 Keep close to the defender as you drive past her and hold your head up as you dribble toward the basket. If you see another defender moving to stop you, try to pass the ball to a teammate.

Protect and keep control of the ball.

Dribble and stop
Practice stopping dribbling and going straight into a jump shot.

Rebound play

A NUMBER OF shots at the basket are missed and rebound off the basket rim or backboard. When this happens, either team can grab the ball. To improve your chance of gaining possession, you need to be well placed in the key area. This involves moving to a position between your opponent and the backboard, or boxing out the opponent. Whether your team is defending or attacking, you will be trying to box out an opponent to be in a good position from which to jump for the rebound.

The ball is heading for the basket.

Avoid the temptation to watch the ball instead of your opponent, since she may take this opportunity to move in for the rebound.

The shooting hand follows the shot through.

Boxing out

When you are boxing out, like the defender in green in this picture sequence, your aim is to act as a barrier between your opponent and the basket. A certain amount of body contact is allowed in boxing out and jumping for rebounds, but you must not push or elbow your opponent or you will be penalized.

The attacker keeps her eyes fixed on the basket.

Keep watching your opponent.

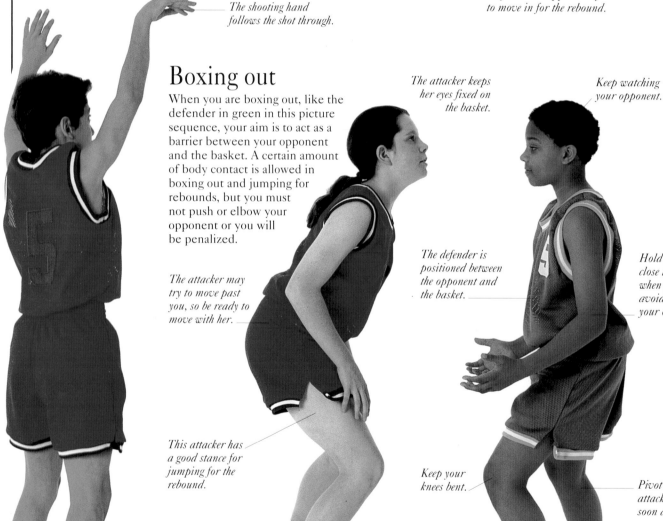

The attacker may try to move past you, so be ready to move with her.

The defender is positioned between the opponent and the basket.

Hold your arms close to your body when you pivot to avoid holding your opponent.

This attacker has a good stance for jumping for the rebound.

Keep your knees bent.

Pivot into the attacker's path as soon as she moves.

The shooter is facing the basket and has used a good shooting technique.

1 When you are defending the basket, you should be facing your opponent, focusing on her movements. As a shot is made, take a step into her path and pivot so you turn your back on her.

Get ready to step into your opponent's path.

When the ball rebounds off the rim, watch its flight carefully.

Hold the ball with both hands.

Pivot so you keep your back to your opponent.

Timing your jump
Learning to time your jump is very important. Wait until the ball has left the basket rim or the backboard before you jump.

Your opponent will be trying to get in a good position for the rebound.

When you jump, swing up your arms and hands to help you lift off the floor.

Feel your opponent at your back, and if she moves, move with her.

Hold up your hands, ready to catch the ball.

Defender catching a rebound
If you catch the rebound while you are defending, you should move the ball out of the key area as quickly as possible. Pass to a teammate near a sideline.

Fouling
Do not push your opponent with your body or hands. This is illegal and can be dangerous.

Stand with your feet shoulder-width apart, knees slightly bent, and head up.

You will need to be at full stretch when you jump for the ball.

If you have space, jump straight back up and shoot.

2 Once you have your opponent facing your back, focus your attention on the ball. Jump for the rebound once you have decided where it will drop. You will want to gain maximum height from your jump. Use your elbows and hands to help give you lift, and reach for the ball with both hands.

Attacker catching a rebound
When you are attacking, you should work hard to get into the boxing out position. If you catch the ball, immediately jump up again and shoot for the basket.

Defense

WHEN YOUR TEAM is defending, it must try to stop the attacking team from getting into a scoring position. There are many tactics you can use, both when defending as a team and as an individual. With individual (one-to-one) defense, you take a position between the opponent you are guarding and the basket you are defending. This will stop your opponent from taking the quickest straight-line route to the basket. Keep pressuring your opponent so that he or she is discouraged from making an attacking move. Try to determine what your opponent might do next, so that you are always prepared.

Defensive stance

When you guard an attacker with the ball, use your hands to block passing lanes. The palms of your hands should face your opponent, since this will make you appear bigger. If you focus your attention on the attacker's waist rather than on the ball, you will find it easier to avoid falling for a fake.

Defending against a dribbler

When your opponent is dribbling the ball, you will need to be agile. Your defensive stance is with knees bent and feet flat on the floor, shoulder-width apart. In this position, you can react quickly to the dribbler's movements. You will have to keep this position against your opponent as you move.

1 Position yourself between your opponent and the basket, taking the defensive stance. As you move with him, your feet should slide across the floor, using a short, shuffling action. By keeping close contact with the floor, you are ready to make quick changes of direction in response to the dribbler.

The dribbler will be looking for an opportunity to drive to the basket.

Keep your feet wide apart and flat on the floor.

2 When the attacker tries to dribble past you, step back from him before moving across into his path. This will give you more time to cover his movements. It will also ensure that you do not make contact with him.

Position your arms so you are ready to steal the ball if the dribbler fails to protect it.

The attacker will be dribbling the ball on the side of his body away from you.

Do not stand too close to your opponent since he will find it easier to dribble past you.

Try not to cross your feet as you move.

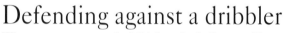

Body contact foul

You can go anywhere on the court as long as you do not cause contact by entering an opponent's personal space. If you touch an opponent you are guarding, you are responsible for that contact and may be penalized. If a dribbler charges into you, the dribbler will be charged with a foul.

Here, the dribbler has run into the defender.

Obstructing with the arm

You are not allowed to stop an opponent's movement by extending your arm to obstruct the opponent. This type of foul is likely to happen if you are tempted to reach across a dribbler's body to try to steal the ball. Even if you avoid making body contact, you could easily lose your balance and be beaten by the dribbler.

The arm is fouling the dribbler.

Personal space

You can occupy any place on the playing court not occupied by an opponent.

3 Keep your hands down near the ball with the palms of your hands facing the dribbler. Look for an opportunity to flick the ball away from the dribbler. Ideally, you should always stay at arm's length from your opponent.

Try to move into a good position in the direction the dribbler wants to go.

Keep facing your opponent.

Palm of the hand is facing the opponent.

Remember to shuffle your feet, taking short steps.

By dribbling the ball close to the floor, the dribbler makes it harder for you to steal the ball.

Team defense

GOOD TEAMWORK is as important when you are on defense as it is when you are on offense. Your team should work together to pressure your opponents, trying to make life difficult for them. This can mean forcing them to make passing errors, intercepting their passes or shots at the basket, or using defense tactics that frustrate them. Learning to defend the area of the court from which your opponents can score is vital. You will need to discourage them from taking a shot within that area by guarding potential shooters closely, and by holding your hands up to block any shots.

Defensive stance
Dikembe Mutombo of the Denver Nuggets takes an excellent defensive stance against David Robinson of the San Antonio Spurs. Mutombo, facing Robinson with his knees bent and hands up to the ball, forces Robinson to pivot away from the basket to protect the ball.

Preventing a pass
Work hard to prevent an attacking player from passing to a teammate close to the basket.

This player is signaling for a pass.

Guarding a passer

When you are guarding an opponent with the ball, do not relax your defense once he or she has passed the ball. Your opponent is still a scoring threat since he or she may cut (move without the ball) to the basket and try to receive the ball to score.

The palms of your hands should face the ball handler.

The player with the ball is called the ball handler.

The ball handler is standing in the triple threat position and has his head up so he can see all his attacking options.

Stand in the basic basketball stance between your opponent and the basket.

1 Hold your arms up and keep moving them. This will make it harder for your opponent to find a passing lane or take a shot. If your opponent has stopped dribbling, you may move closer to him because he cannot start a second dribble. This will put him under more pressure.

Good defense
Remember – good defending means using your feet to stay in position and using your brain to figure out what your opponent may do next.

Preventing pass reception

When you are guarding an attacker close to the basket who wants the ball, you can try to prevent them from receiving the ball. To do this, move your defensive position from between your opponent and the basket to stand at the side of your opponent nearest the ball handler. Hold up one arm to block a passing lane. In this position you should be able to see both your opponent and the person with the ball. This defensive action is called "overplaying" the opponent.

Possession time limit
Depending on your league, your opponents only have a certain amount of time in which to take a shot, usually around 30 seconds. If you can prevent your opponents from shooting within this time, your team will gain possession.

Keep both opponents in your sight.

Be careful not to obstruct your opponent with your arm.

The ball is positioned for an overhead pass.

One of your teammates will be responsible for guarding the ball handler.

Your opponent will be trying to break away from you.

Keep your feet wide apart.

Try to force the ball handler to pass to a teammate away from the basket.

The pass receiver is preparing to shoot.

Keep your arms up to discourage a pass behind you to another attacker.

Be aware of the ball
Look at a point halfway between your opponent and the person with the ball. This way you are aware of where the ball is, without losing sight of your opponent.

After passing, your opponent may try to cut to the basket.

Take one step back from your opponent so you have more time to cover his movements.

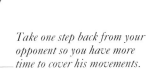

The attacker follows through with his hands as he makes the pass.

Keep your feet wide apart as you may need to move quickly in any direction.

2 When your opponent makes a pass to a teammate, you will need to change your defensive position. You must continue guarding him in case he moves to receive a return pass. Make sure you stay aware of where the ball is and where your opponent is standing.

Keep your eyes fixed on the ball.

Reach for the ball with the palm of your hand facing toward you.

Note the positions of your teammates so you can try to tip the ball to one of them.

Restarting play

THERE ARE many times during a basketball game when play is stopped by an official, such as when a player commits a foul or a ball goes out of bounds. The way the game is restarted depends on why it was stopped. To start the game and each five-minute period of overtime, a jump ball is used. It is also used to restart the game in some other circumstances, one of which is when the ball gets lodged in the basket supports. A throw-in is another method of restarting play. This is used when the ball goes over a boundary line, or if play has stopped because a player has broken a rule. In some instances when a player is fouled, free throws are awarded to that player's team. A free throw is a shot at the basket taken from the free throw line, with no player allowed in the key area while the shot is being taken.

Lineup at jump ball

For a jump ball to start a game, which is also called a tip-off, one player from each team stands in the center circle on the side of the half-court line nearest to their own team's basket. Only the two players involved in the jump ball are allowed in the center circle. The other players will usually stand close to the circle so that they are in a good position to catch the ball if it is tipped toward them.

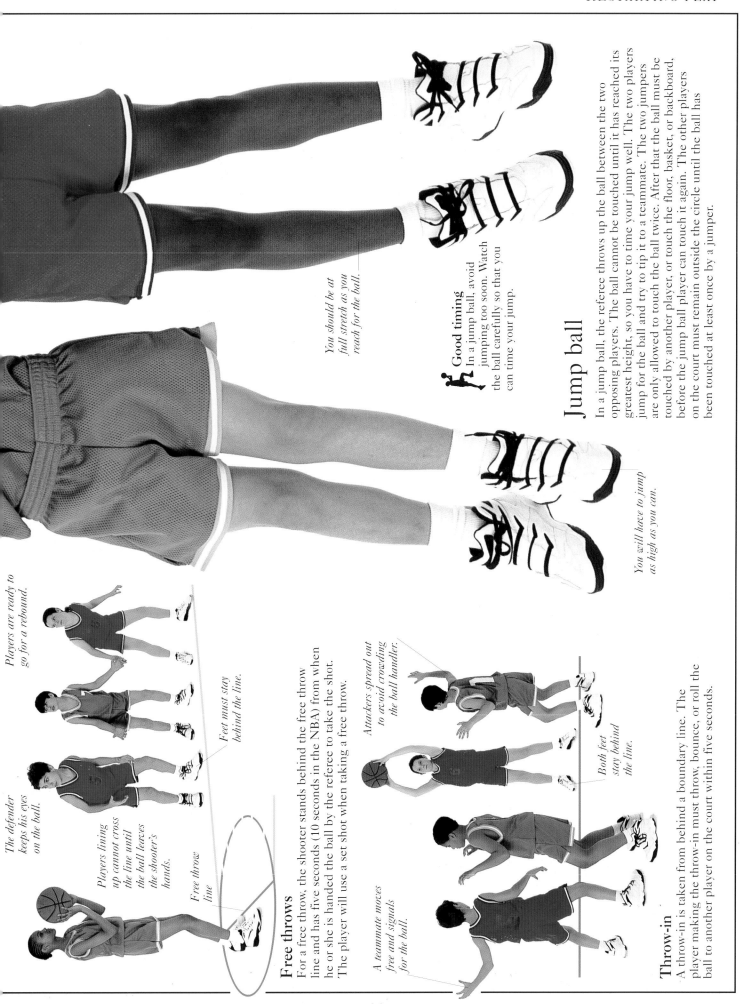

You should be at full stretch as you reach for the ball.

Good timing
In a jump ball, avoid jumping too soon. Watch the ball carefully so that you can time your jump.

Jump ball

In a jump ball, the referee throws up the ball between the two opposing players. The ball cannot be touched until it has reached its greatest height, so you have to time your jump well. The two players jump for the ball and try to tip it to a teammate. The two jumpers are only allowed to touch the ball twice. After that the ball must be touched by another player, or touch the floor, basket, or backboard, before the jump ball player can touch it again. The other players on the court must remain outside the circle until the ball has been touched at least once by a jumper.

You will have to jump as high as you can.

Players are ready to go for a rebound.

The defender keeps his eyes on the ball.

Feet must stay behind the line.

Players lining up cannot cross the line until the ball leaves the shooter's hands.

Free throw line

Free throws
For a free throw, the shooter stands behind the free throw line and has five seconds (10 seconds in the NBA) from when he or she is handed the ball by the referee to take the shot. The player will use a set shot when taking a free throw.

A teammate moves free and signals for the ball.

Attackers spread out to avoid crowding the ball handler.

Both feet stay behind the line.

Throw-in
A throw-in is taken from behind a boundary line. The player making the throw-in must throw, bounce, or roll the ball to another player on the court within five seconds.

Positional play

E VERY PLAYER in a basketball game can handle the ball and is free to move anywhere on the court. Because of this, playing positions must be organized, or players on the same team might get in each other's way. The position that you play on the court will depend upon your skills, your height and physical ability, and the tactics your coach uses. There are three basic playing positions – guard, forward, and center. These positions are related to the area of the court from which you operate when your team is on offense, and you may change playing positions during a game.

Team defensive play

This diagram shows the simplest form of team defense, one-to-one defense, in which each defensive player is responsible for guarding one opponent. If you are guarding the ball handler, stand about 3 ft (1 m) away from him or her. If your opponent does not have the ball, stand so that you can see both the ball and your opponent. In addition to changing your stance, you should move farther away from your opponent. The farther your opponent is away from the ball, the farther you should be from your opponent.

Defending area
Remember that your team's defensive effort will be concentrated on the area of the court from which an attacker has a good chance of scoring.

Starting positions

Your coach will decide on which positions you and your teammates should take to ensure that your team is spread out. The positions taken by you and your teammates will depend on your individual strengths and the tactics of your opponents.

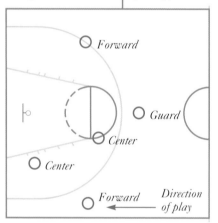

Playing positions

The player in the guard position is usually the smallest and fastest member of the team. Guards play in the area of the court between the half-court and the free throw lines. They need to be good ball handlers, excellent dribblers and passers, and skilled long-range shooters. A forward is usually taller than a guard, but not as tall as a center. Forwards play at the side of the court between the free throw line and the sideline. They should be good scorers from the side of the court and should try to catch offensive rebounds. Centers are usually the tallest players and play closest to the basket. They must be good at catching rebounds and scoring close to the basket.

Notice that I have my head up as I dribble, using the hand farthest from my defender.

1-3-1 formation
In this formation you have one guard, two forwards, and one center in a line, and one center close to the basket you are attacking.

Dribbling
Dribbling is good for moving the ball up the court or for getting away from a defender. Here I am using my dribble to move past my defender and get closer to the basket.

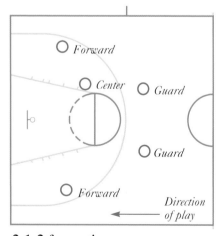

When posting up, use a jump stop to land with knees bent.

Posting up
You will need to develop the ability to move free ahead of the ball handler. Centers frequently use a move called "posting up" to get free from their defender to receive a pass. In this move the center starts from a position close to the basket and then runs toward the free throw line to receive the ball. Since the defender will be between the center and the basket, moving away from the basket makes it difficult for the defender to intercept the pass.

2-1-2 formation
The 2-1-2 is the simplest formation with two guards, one center, and two forwards. Players are evenly spread around the basket.

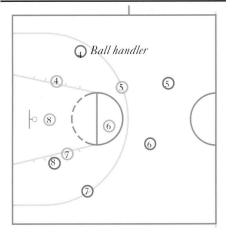

Ball handler

Red number 4 has the ball and is closely guarded by green number 4.

Green defenders 5 and 6 have moved away from their opponents, red 5 and 6, who do not have the ball.

Rebounding

This picture shows the Charlotte Hornets (in blue) using one-to-one defense against the New York Knicks (in white). The Hornet's Larry Johnson is catching a rebound.

Magic Johnson displays an excellent defensive stance against John Stockton.

Arms held out to block a shot or pass

The Hornets have achieved good positions close to the basket.

In this picture, my style is good as I take a jump shot.

Shooting

The moment you receive a pass anywhere on the court you should pivot to face the basket you are attacking. Provided you have brought the ball into the triple threat position, you should be able to decide quickly if you have space and are in range to shoot. If you can shoot and have a defender between you and the basket, you can take a set shot or a jump shot.

Remember to release the ball at the top of your jump.

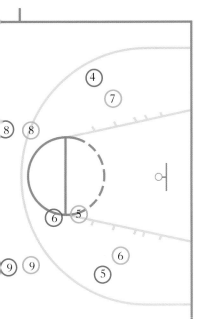

Diagram

This diagram shows an example of playing positions of attackers (red circles) and defenders (green). Any of the positions are within attacking range, although it would be risky for attackers 8 and 9 to shoot as they are far from the basket. When posting up, you may be at attacking player 6's position when you receive the ball.

Hold your head up and decide on your best offensive option.

Attack the basket

Whenever you receive the ball in your opponent's half of the court, you must learn to position yourself quickly so you can attack the basket. Remember to take up the triple threat position, threatening to shoot, dribble, or pass the ball.

Catch the ball with both hands.

1 If you are being guarded, break free from your defender and signal for the ball. When you catch it, come to a legal stop and pivot to face the basket.

2 From your triple threat position, you need to decide if you should shoot, dribble the ball closer to the basket, or pass to a free teammate.

Keep your knees bent and be ready to move quickly.

Fast break

THE MOMENT your team gets the ball, whether from a rebound or an interception, it should break for the basket as quickly as possible. As your team attacks, the opposing team will be trying to reset their defense, so you must quickly move the ball within scoring range before your opponents have time to recover. The team attack shown here, called a fast break, is one of the most exciting aspects of the game for both players and spectators. The aim is to move the ball down the court so that you outnumber the opposition and create a chance to score.

Attacker running down the right

Attacker running down the left

The defender is chasing the dribbler.

Dribbler

Three lane attack

When your team starts a fast break, the ball handler should dribble down the middle of the court. Meanwhile, two other attackers should sprint toward the basket, one on each side of the court so that the attack is moving down three lanes. This move gives the dribbler a choice of receivers if he or she cannot go directly to the basket to score.

How to fast break

When you are fast breaking and your attackers outnumber the defenders, try to commit a defender to guarding you by dribbling straight to the basket. This should leave a teammate free to receive the ball and take a shot at the basket.

Fast break speed
Practice running at speed down the court while dribbling and passing the ball between teammates.

The defender stays between the dribbler and the basket.

The teammate is signaling for the ball.

1 In this sequence, the ball handler is dribbling the ball toward the basket, forcing defender number 4 to commit himself to guarding her. The dribbler's teammate is left open and is running toward the basket, signaling for a pass.

The defender must do his best to delay the dribbler, giving his teammates time to get back to defend the basket.

Keep control of the ball
The success of a fast break depends on moving the ball down the court quickly. Avoid going too fast in case you lose control, and consequently possession of the ball.

The defender has been beaten by the fast break.

The passer throws the ball.

The receiver can take the ball and dribble up to the basket.

Outlet pass

David Robinson catches the rebound from a missed shot while his teammates run out from defense to start a fast break. They are ready for Robinson's outlet pass, which is a quick pass made by a defender from the key area out to the side of the court.

Pass ahead

Players without the ball can run faster than a player dribbling the ball. When your team is fast breaking, the ball handler should look to pass to a teammate closer to the opponent's basket than he or she is. The ball should be thrown ahead of the receiver so it can be caught without slowing the receiver's running speed.

Fouled shooter

If the shooter scores but is fouled by the defender while in the act of shooting, the attacking team will get two points for the basket and will also get a free throw for the foul.

Once the defender is beaten, he will have to recover his defensive position to defend the shot.

2 The defender has his arms outstretched to discourage the dribbler from passing the ball. The dribbler sees a passing lane and makes a bounce pass. Once she has passed the ball, she cuts to the basket.

3 The receiver is near the basket and takes a layup shot. The defender is putting pressure on the shooter by keeping his arms up and following the shooter in on the layup.

Both hands are held out ready to catch the ball.

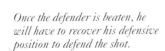

The shooter raises his knee to give him extra lift.

The receiver should keep moving, either by dribbling or going into a layup.

Give and go

EVERY TIME your team is on offense, you will be trying to convert your attack into a good shot at the basket. A scoring opportunity may be created by an individual player, or it may involve two or three players cooperating so that one of them is able to take a shot. The "give and go" is a simple and effective offensive move involving two players working together. One attacker passes, or gives, the ball to a teammate. The giver then cuts, or goes, to the basket, signaling to receive a return pass and score.

Hands held out for the ball

Push off the left foot.

Change of direction

When you are looking to receive the ball, making a quick change of direction is very useful for fooling defenders. For instance, move to the left and, as a defender reacts to your move, push off your left foot to go to the right. If, as you change direction, you also change your speed from slow to fast, you will find it easier to lose your opponent.

Give and go

When you make the give pass, you will find it more effective if the teammate receiving the ball is closer to the basket than you are. When you have passed the ball, your defender will often relax slightly because you are no longer a scoring threat. At this moment you should attack and cut in for the return pass.

Pass the ball using both hands.

2 When the receiver catches the ball, she quickly pivots to face the basket. The giver fools his defender with a fake. He moves to his left and, when the defender moves to cover, the giver quickly changes direction.

1 The giver, red number 4, passes to a teammate who has moved away from her defender. The giver will cut toward the basket, trying to free himself from his defender.

The giver drives hard off his left foot.

The ball handler threatens to shoot.

Backdoor cut

When you are close to the basket and want to receive the ball, your defender may overplay you by standing in the direct passing lane between you and the ball handler. To beat your defender, you can use a "backdoor cut." This is when you break away from the side of your defender farthest from the ball handler.

The attacker holds up her hand as if she is trying to receive the ball.

The defender tries to see both his opponent and the ball handler.

1 Move out in the direction of the ball handler as if you are trying to receive the ball. Your defender will move with you.

The defender moves with the attacker.

The defender is caught off balance.

Hand signal

2 Quickly change direction, moving away from the defender and the ball handler. Cut to the basket, signaling for the ball.

The attacker runs to receive the ball.

Give and go position

This diagram shows the position of the two attacking players, red numbers 4 and 6, and their defenders at the beginning of the picture sequence across these two pages. This position is excellent for executing the give and go.

Where to give and go
You can use the give and go anywhere on the court. It does not have to end with a shot at the basket.

4 The giver is close enough to the basket to go straight into a lay-up shot. He has moved so fast that his defender has not had time to get between him and the basket.

3 The giver beats his defender and cuts to the basket. The ball handler passes to the giver when she sees he has freed himself from his defender. The pass is made ahead of the giver so he can catch the ball on the run.

The defender is left behind.

The ball handler makes an overhead pass.

The giver cuts close to the defender and moves straight to the basket.

Show your intentions
When you make the give, quickly cut toward the basket and indicate clearly to the ball handler where you want to receive the ball.

The attacker is at full stretch to make the layup.

39

Screen play

SCREEN PLAY is a tactic in which an attacker obstructs, or creates a screen against, a defender guarding another offensive player. The purpose of a screen is to help a teammate lose a defender so he or she can make a shot, drive to the basket, or cut to receive a pass. Screen play is an occasion when two attackers will move close together and not keep their usual 10-13 ft (3-4 m) distance apart. It is not illegal for an attacker in a screen and a defender to make body contact, unless excessive force is used by either player to beat the opponent.

Screen away from the ball

A screen is not only used to free a player with the ball. When you are on offense, you should be prepared to set a pick on the defender of a teammate who does not have the ball. This would free your teammate to receive a pass and either dribble to the basket or go straight into a shot. In this picture, red number 4 has set a pick for his teammate number 5, who has been able to cut past his defender to receive a pass from number 6.

Pick screen

A pick screen involves two teammates working together to free one of them from his or her defender. In this sequence, a pick is set along the path that a defender is trying to follow. The attacker who sets the pick obstructs the defender's progress as she guards the ball handler, giving the ball handler a chance to dribble to the basket.

Screening stance
A player who is screening an opponent should be stationary and have both feet flat on the floor.

The defender is standing between his opponent and the basket.

The defender is closely guarding the attacker.

The ball handler fakes a dribble to the left.

The attackers are 10-13 ft (3-4 m) apart when they start the move.

This defender is in a good defensive stance.

The attacker steps into the pass to achieve a greater distance with the throw.

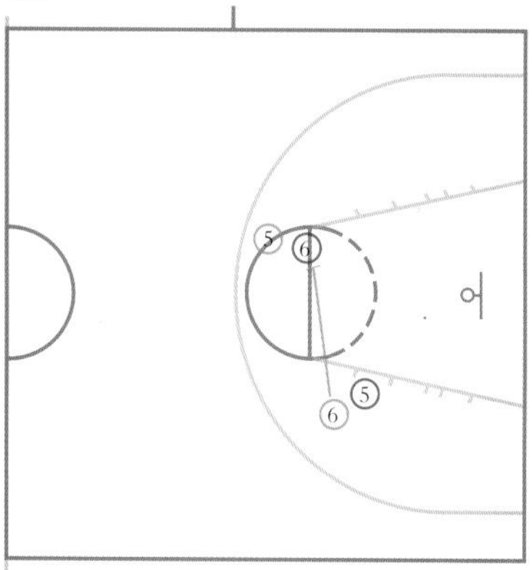

Pick screen positions
This diagram shows the position taken by the two attackers at stage 1 of the picture sequence. The green line shows the path green number 6 will take to screen her teammate's defender.

1 A player passes to her teammate who has moved free. When the receiver catches the ball, he will pivot to face the basket, watching the movements of his teammate.

Attacker setting the pick

Defender of red number 4

Hand signals for the ball

Number 5 moved close to the screen as he ran past.

Attacker setting the pick

This defender slides through the gap.

This defender steps away from the attacker he is guarding.

Defending a screen

You may find yourself guarding an attacker who is screening one of your teammates. Let your teammate know about the attacker setting the pick and step back to give your teammate space to move between you and the screen. This move is called sliding. You may help your teammate by pulling him or her through the gap.

The dribbler is moving toward the basket.

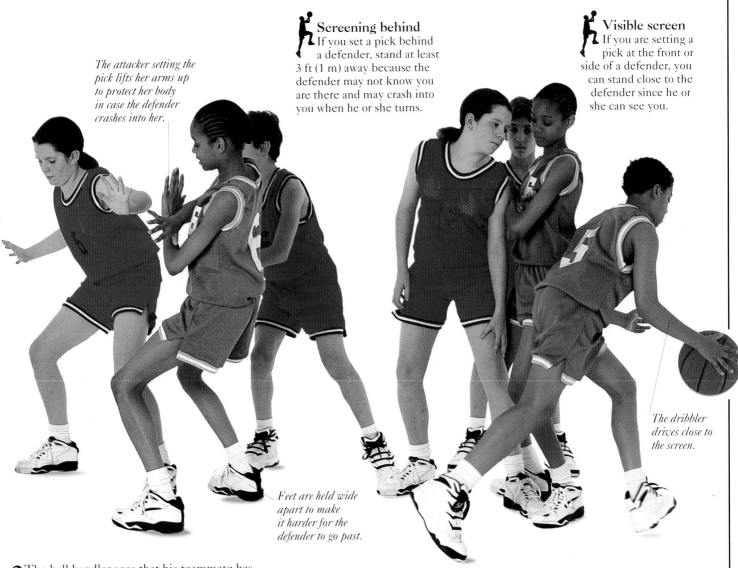

Screening behind

If you set a pick behind a defender, stand at least 3 ft (1 m) away because the defender may not know you are there and may crash into you when he or she turns.

Visible screen

If you are setting a pick at the front or side of a defender, you can stand close to the defender since he or she can see you.

The attacker setting the pick lifts her arms up to protect her body in case the defender crashes into her.

Feet are held wide apart to make it harder for the defender to go past.

The dribbler drives close to the screen.

2 The ball handler sees that his teammate has moved close and has taken a position in the path where the defender would go if the ball handler dribbled to the basket. The ball handler, in order to distract the defender from his teammate setting the pick, fakes to dribble to his left.

3 The ball handler changes direction and dribbles to the right, moving close to the screen. The defender tries to follow the dribbler but has to check her movement because of the screen. The attacker who set the pick will hold position until the defender makes contact with her.

Leagues

BASKETBALL IS ONE of the most popular sports in the world, and leagues are organized for different age groups and all levels of performance. As your game improves, you can play on a team at your school or in a local club, competing against other local teams. Eventually, you might reach the highest level leagues, in which there are international and national tournaments. Or you could play for the biggest basketball league in the world, the NBA, which has 27 professional teams. But whether you find yourself playing or simply watching, basketball is always exciting.

Wheelchair basketball
Wheelchair basketball is very similar to the regular game, which is called the running game by those who play in wheelchairs. Most of the rules are the same, although there are different rules for dribbling. As in regular basketball, players need to pass, dribble, defend, and shoot. The game starts with a tip-off, scoring is the same, and time regulations are similar.

Special wheelchairs
Players in the wheelchair league usually play in specially built sports wheelchairs, like the ones in this picture, that are easy to maneuver.

Rules and regulations
The international rules of the game and all international competitions are controlled by the International Basketball Federation (FIBA). Every country in which basketball is a sport has its own basketball federation that is responsible for controlling the sport within that country. There are approximately 200 countries affiliated with the FIBA. In the US, the NBA and the NCAA (American college league) use rules that differ slightly from the FIBA rules.

International program

Olympic Games
These are held every four years for both men's and women's teams.

World Championships
There are six World Championships, each held every four years:
- Men: 16 teams take part.
- Women: 16 teams take part.
- Junior men: 16 teams take part. Players must be aged 18 or younger.
- Men 22 years and under. This is a new competition and is designed to provide a transition from junior to senior level.

- Men's wheelchair basketball: first held in 1973.
- Women's wheelchair basketball: first held in 1990.

For all these World Championships, the host countries gain automatic entry. In addition to world competitions, FIBA organizes competitions through seven zones – Africa, Asia, North America, Central America, South America, Europe, and Oceania. FIBA also organizes competitions in these zones for players aged 16 or younger, who are called cadet players.

NBA game
Here I am playing in an NBA game against an opponent who is guarding me closely. I have timed my drive well so that I have space to move in for a shot at the basket.

Basketball for young players
To help promote the game for young people, the FIBA has published a set of rules to be used by 14-year-olds and under. These are called the Passerelle Rules. In addition, there is a worldwide movement to promote basketball for 12-year-olds and under. This is the "mini-basketball" movement, and it provides rules and tournaments in most countries. In mini-basketball, boys and girls play on the same team. In recent years there has been an increase in the popularity of three versus three tournaments (three players to a team). These provide an opportunity for young players to compete against players of similar ability, and offer excellent grounding for those just starting to play.

Women's basketball
Women started to play basketball in the early 1890s, and women's basketball has been included in the Olympic Games since 1976. This picture shows a jump ball at the start of an Olympic match between China and the CIS (Commonwealth of Independent States).

Glossary

During basketball practice, or when watching basketball, you may find it helpful to understand some of the following words and phrases.

A

Air ball When the ball is shot so poorly that it does not hit the rim.

Assist A pass to a teammate that leads directly to a basket.

B

Backcourt The half of a court that a team is defending.

Baseline The boundary line underneath each basket.

Baseline drive A very fast dribble made close to the boundary line underneath the basket that is being attacked.

Basket The goal, and also the name for a score.

Blocking out Another name for boxing out.

Boxing out The position taken by a player at a rebound to stop an opponent from getting near the basket.

C

Crossover dribble Bouncing the ball very quickly from one hand to the other.

Cut A fast movement made by an attacking player without the ball toward the opposing team's basket.

D

Dead ball A ball that is not in play because of a rule infringement, a goal being scored, or because it has gone over a boundary line.

Double team Two defenders guarding an attacker who has the ball.

Drive A fast and aggressive dribble toward the opposing team's basket.

Dunk When a player jumps up and pushes the ball through the basket from above.

E

Endline Another name for the baseline.

F

Fake When you pretend to move one way and then move in another direction in order to force an opponent off balance.

Field goal A goal scored from open play (as opposed to a free throw) worth two or three points depending on where the shooter was standing when he or she took the shot.

Free throw An undefended shot awarded to a team because of a foul by an opponent. A free throw is taken from behind the free throw line.

Frontcourt The half of a court that a team is attacking.

Full-court press A defensive tactic used over the whole court.

H

Half-court press A defensive tactic used in the half of the court a team is defending.

Held ball When two or more opposing players have both of their hands firmly on the ball.

High percentage shot A shot taken by a player when there is a very high chance that he or she will score.

J

Jump ball When the ball is thrown up by the referee between two opponents to start or restart play.

K

Key The restricted area and semicircle around the baskets at each end of the court.

L

"L" cut When an attacking player makes a 90° turn to try and lose a defender.

M

Match up When an attacker and a defender guard each other throughout the game.

O

One-on-one One attacker versus one defender.

One-to-one One defender guarding one attacker.

Options The range of offensive moves available to a player during a game.

Outside shot A shot at the basket taken from outside the area where the defenders are positioned.

Overtime The extra time played when the scores are equal at full time. Play continues in five minute periods until one of the teams wins.

P

Point guard The guard player who is responsible for organizing his team's attacking play.

Post Another name for a center player.

R

Rebound When a missed shot rebounds off the rim or the backboard and is caught by either an attacker or a defender.

S

Sag When defenders move away from their opponents toward the basket that is being defended.

Screen A play in which an attacking player takes a position to stop an opponent from continuing to guard a teammate.

Slam Another name for a dunk.

Squaring up Positioning yourself so you face the basket.

Steal Taking the ball from your opponent.

Stuff Another name for a dunk.

Swish shot A shot that goes through the basket without touching the rim or backboard.

Switch A defensive move in which two defenders swap attackers they are guarding.

T

Throw-in A way of restarting play by throwing the ball in from a boundary line. The throw-in is used to restart play after a rule infringement. It is also awarded to a team if the opposition goes over the time limit for possession of the ball, or when the opposition puts the ball out of bounds.

Tip-off Another name for a jump ball.

Traveling When a player takes more than the legal amount of steps while holding the ball.

Turnover When one team loses possession of the ball without having taken a shot.

V

"V" cut An attacking move. The player takes two or three steps forward and then changes direction to move out and receive a pass. By doing this, the player moves in a "V" shape.

W

Weak side The side of the court where the offensive team does not have the ball.

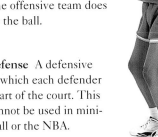

Z

Zone defense A defensive tactic in which each defender guards part of the court. This tactic cannot be used in mini-basketball or the NBA.

More basketball rules

30 second rule – the attacking team must take a shot within 30 seconds of gaining possession of the ball (24 seconds in the NBA, and 35 seconds in the NCAA).

10 second rule – when a team has the ball in its own half of the court, it has 10 seconds to move the ball into the opponent's half.

5 second rule – a player must make a throw-in within 5 seconds. Under FIBA rules a free throw must be taken within 5 seconds as well (10 seconds in the NBA).

3 second rule – an attacking player is not permitted to stand in the opponent's restricted (key) area for longer than 3 seconds.

Personal foul – an infringement of the rules that involves body contact with an opponent.

Technical foul – when a player or a coach is penalized for bad behavior, such as arguing with the referee. If a player or coach receives two technical fouls, he or she will be ejected from the game.

Disqualifying foul – an unsportsmanlike foul on another player, such as a punch, for which a player is ejected from the game.

Five fouls rule – a player who commits five fouls, whether personal or technical, (six personal fouls in the NBA), must be replaced and take no further part in the game.

Violation – a rule infringement that is not a personal or a technical foul. The main violations are: an illegal dribble; traveling; spending more than three seconds in the restricted area; being responsible for the ball going out of bounds.

Player out of bounds – A player is out of bounds if he or she touches a boundary line or the area outside the line.

Ball out of bounds – the ball is out of bounds when a player with the ball, or the ball itself, touches a boundary line or the area outside the line. A ball in the air is not out of bounds until it touches the floor on or outside the line.

Goal-tending rule – a player is not permitted to touch the ball when it is on its downward flight toward a basket. A defender may not touch the ball when it is in the basket.

Backcourt violation – once a team has moved the ball from their half of the court (the backcourt) to the opposing team's half (the frontcourt), they may not move the ball over the half-court line back into their own half.

Index

Useful addresses

Here are the addresses of some basketball associations and athletic organizations that you may find useful. They may be able to help you find a local league to join so you can start playing with a team, and they can provide some guidance in terms of official rules and play in different basketball leagues. Be sure to check with your school as well – it may be affiliated with a local league you can join right away.

Amateur Athletic Union of the US
3400 West 86th Street
PO Box 68207
Indianapolis, Indiana 46268
(317) 357-8790

National Federation of State High School Associations
11724 Northwest Plaza Circle
Kansas City, Missouri 64195
(816) 464-5400

National Collegiate Athletic Association (NCAA)
620 College Drive
Overland Park, Kansas 66211
(913) 339-1906

National Basketball Association (NBA)
Olympic Tower Building
645 Fifth Avenue
New York, New York 10022
(212) 407 8000

US Olympic Committee
1 Olympic Plaza
Colorado Springs, Colorado 80909
(719) 632-5551

Basketball Canada
1600 James Naismith Drive
Suite 715
Gloucester, Ontario
K1B 5N4
(613) 748 5607

Mark   Martin

Lauren

Chelsee

Lendel

Kieron

Acknowledgments

Dorling Kindersley would like to thank the following people
for their help in the production of this book:

All the Young Players for their skill and enthusiasm during the photographic sessions; Joe White, basketball coach at Homerton House School, London and Tony Garbelotto of London Towers, for providing the players and for the practical advice and assistance offered; Sportserve for making the team uniforms and for the loan of the basketball equipment.

Picture credits
key: B bottom; L left; R right; C center; T top; a above; b below.

Action Plus/S. Bardens: 10BL
Allsport/S. Bruty: 42BR; T. Defrisco: 8BL, 30TC, 37TL; S. Dunn: 8CR; O. Greule: 42BL; M. Powell: 9BL,9BR British Sports Association for the Disabled/ Graham Bool: 42TR

Colorsport/16TR; Duomo: 34CR, 35C, 35TR; Empics: back jacket; D. Madison: 12TR; P.J. Sutton: 35TC
Naismith Memorial Basketball Hall of Fame: 9TR, 9CLa, 9CLb, 9CR Range/Bettmann/UPI: 9C
Sporting Pictures: 8TL, 8BR, 8C, 12BL, 24TR, 25TL